Finding Myself
SOBER

DEAN S. ANDERSON

Fulton Books
Meadville, PA

Published by Fulton Books 2023

ISBN 979-8-88731-079-4 (paperback)
ISBN 979-8-88731-080-0 (digital)

Printed in the United States of America

Contents

Preface...v

Chapter 1: Honesty 1

Chapter 2: Hope..8

Chapter 3: Faith..15

Chapter 4: Courage 24

Chapter 5: Integrity 32

Chapter 6: Willingness...39

Chapter 7: Humility 46

Chapter 8: Love 53

Chapter 9: Responsibility.....................................61

Chapter 10: Discipline...68

Chapter 11: Spirituality 75

Chapter 12: Service...84

Conclusion...91

Preface

This is the second book I have written. The first book was based on what I have learned over my life about relationships. I bring this up because I could not have written that book if it were not for the principles listed in this new book. Let me start by saying that I am forty-eight and got sober when I was thirty-nine. I have nine continuous years of sobriety as of February 7, 2022. I am forever grateful for my sobriety, and it couldn't have been accomplished without many factors, one of which is being active in a twelve-step program.

I believe we all start off as good people, what God created us to be. Somewhere along the way, we pick up bad habits or we get hurt by certain people or we pick up these unrealistic fears that drive our behaviors. We try to find the solutions to these issues in many unhealthy ways. For me, that unhealthy way was drinking alcohol. I loved it the moment I drank it. It seemed to temporarily solve all my problems. Where I lacked in life, alcohol made up for it and made me the person I thought I wanted to be. Well, at some point in time, it turned on me as it does on so many. I was at the stage where there was no going back and my drinking had taken me to a life-or-death situation. I had hurt and worried many around me, and it was time to stop. I wasn't ready to meet my Creator yet.

Simply put, I was sick and tired of being sick and tired. I was an embarrassment to myself and many loved ones at the end. So I went to a treatment center and I was reintroduced to a twelve-step program that saved my life. Let me point out that the cessation of drinking does not solve your problems for a true alcoholic. The biggest issue is with my alcoholic mind. I had to reprogram my brain with a lot of help. I wasn't raised to act like I was acting. I almost didn't resemble anything I originally was before I started on this journey with alcohol, which for me started around thirteen years old. I had a great upbringing and great parents, and I grew up in a great town in Massachusetts.

Now that I was able to stop drinking, it was time to get back to what God originally created me to be, albeit with a little more life experience than I had at thirteen when I decided to take up my relationship with the bottle. This book is based on twelve spiritual principles that were the catalyst to me hitting that reset button. These life-saving principles allowed me to find myself again, grow into something new and confident, and become what God had wanted me to be all along.

I'm grateful for that journey that I went through, even for the rock bottom I eventually hit. It's a grave reminder about how I never want to go back to that way of life again. It's now about how I want to live in abundance and gratitude. I'm writing this book as a recovered alcoholic that got myself centered and found spirituality through these principles. However, I'm of the opinion that these principles can apply to anyone with any problem anywhere in the world. So here are twelve chapters to dive into *Finding Myself Sober*. I hope it helps someone as much as it helps me to live a new and wonderful life.

CHAPTER 1
Honesty

The first principle of honesty is paramount in recovery because we can only make progress when we are able to be completely truthful with ourselves and others about our issues.

When do you think we start lying? That could mean lying to ourselves or lying to our parents or siblings when we're a little kid. I think it may be different for everyone, but it certainly starts at a very young age. I imagine we start lying to get what we want from our parents. Maybe we lie to a sibling so we can get our way or prevent them from taking something we already have in our possession. Lies are a strange thing because it becomes such a habit that we don't even know we're doing it. I imagine the only lie worth telling at all is the one that is to prevent someone's feelings from getting hurt. That's probably much less a lie than it is just changing the blunt truth a little to package it differently and save someone from getting crushed by a comment. We also have to think of lies by omission. Isn't it still a lie when we withhold the truth? Lying seems to almost become part of who we are to either protect ourselves or possibly protect someone else.

But haven't you ever noticed that lying gets increasingly difficult the more you do it? You start to lie more and more just to cover up other lies that you've told earlier. You often forget who the hell you lied to, so it spins out of control. My wife is a horrible liar, so she probably suffered less with this than I did. By this, I mean that she has no talent or ability to lie. Watching her tell a lie is almost humorous. She was born with the inability to not be honest with others. She can probably be dishonest with herself and manipulate herself to believe in something that may not be true. But lying to others, it's not her game and I love her for that.

Someone close to me once told me I was one of the best liars she had ever met. It wasn't a compliment, though she did say it in humor. I just got really convincing when doing it to cover my own ass over the years, especially related to my alcohol consumption. Let's just say I had broken the occasional law as a kid and out of fear and the possible consequences, I got really good at lying.

Now picture getting sober, and the first principle taught to you in order to create a better life is to always be honest. That doesn't happen overnight. You truly have to be aware of what you say and how you say it. It takes a while. I mean to seriously never lie at all? That seemed near impossible. As an alcoholic, we seem to grow into one big walking lie. This could be a lie to ourselves to try and convince us that we don't have a problem. Or it can be lying about reasons we can't be somewhere because in reality, we're just too far gone and intoxicated to show up. Or we lie to our family and friends about how much we're actually drinking. You know the old comeback when a doctor asks how much alcohol you consume daily. It's always "No more than a six-pack." I mean we *can't* say we're not drinking as our liver enzymes and high blood pressure tell them otherwise. But God forbid, we tell them the truth! That would be much too embarrassing, or even worse, they may tell us we need to stop drinking!

Well, I can tell you that nine years later, I'm getting awfully close to never telling lies at all. I still struggle with lies by omission. I have to catch myself sometimes and correct it immediately. I also try to avoid any white lies, too, as they normally grow into bigger lies. I have found myself on more than one occasion, coming clean to someone immediately after telling a lie and admitting to them what I just did. Can you imagine how embarrassing that is? It will make you not want to do that again. But it's worth the embarrassment to now live a true life, a life where I'm no longer hiding, a life where I shine light into any dark places that are left in me. The fear is too great to risk lying my ass back into a bottle.

Maybe your problem is drugs, food, relationships, or shopping. I believe all these human issues cause us to be dishonest in some way or another. If honesty is the best policy, then start being 100 percent truthful now. Start retraining your brain and calling yourself out on your own bullshit as you go. It's humbling. How great a feeling it is to stop running away from the truth. As it says in the Bible, the truth will set you free. I find it to be the ultimate way to freedom.

If you're living right and you're honest in all areas of your life, you never have to hide from anyone or anything again. One of the definitions of truth is this: a fact or belief that is accepted as true. A fact?

What a concept! Imagine if we spoke in just facts or truth. Wow, what a world we could live in together.

How free do you want to be?

1. How many times do you think you lie per day?
2. Are you willing to count how many lies you told today? Or yesterday?
3. Are you also willing to call yourself out on a lie the moment you tell it?
4. How big is the desire you have to be truthful every day to people around you?
5. Do you lead a double life?
6. Do you care too much about what people think of you?
7. Has lying affected your life negatively?
8. Have you ever been caught in a lie? How did that make you feel?

Space to reflect on
honesty questions.

"How great a
feeling it is to
stop running away
from the truth."

_____

_____

_____

_____

_____

CHAPTER 2
Hope

Remember that line from *The Shawshank Redemption*? Andy Dufresne said, "HOPE is a good thing, maybe the best of things, and no good thing ever dies." What a powerful statement. That quote hit me hard then, and it never left me.

Have you ever felt truly hopeless? I have, or at least I think I have. An alcoholic has a bit of a warped mind. I heard once that alcoholics are egomaniacs with an inferiority complex. That is such a good description. We're one of the few types of people that when in our disease, we can be lying in the gutter but still look down at other people. But then we get sober! This allows us to have hope. I felt truly hopeless when I was at rock bottom from my drinking. My family didn't know what to do with me. I was financially falling apart, I was physically and mentally ill at that time, and I was spiritually bankrupt. My family felt they couldn't help me, and they were right. I could only help myself.

That moment when you first have hope again happened in two different scenarios for me. The first was when I met up with some other alcoholics that I explained my story to and they didn't judge me. They truly accepted me because they, too, had been there and understood. I had hope because they had gotten sober, which meant I could do it too. The second moment was when I had a few weeks sober and I started to laugh again and heard others laughing as well. Very few people in this world, in my opinion, except for people in recovery, can find humor in past misery or laugh at something tragic that has now been reformed. It's a magical moment in an alcoholic's life. It proves to us that we can be human again. For me, it was at about forty-five days when suddenly it dawned on me that I had not thought of alcohol for a couple of days. That's a miracle in itself.

I think during our drinking days, hope is fleeting and it's usually for all the wrong reasons. How many times have you been pulled over by the cops and all you can hope for is to be let go and sent on your way? How many times have you lain on the floor in your bathroom after puking and just hope that the feeling goes away? You may even promise yourself that you'll never drink again. There will be times you hope that no one ever knows how weak you really are or how much you drink in private. These are all false hopes that are sometimes attached to what we call foxhole prayers. They're not genuine. They're delusional, which seems to come with an alcoholic mind. Here, I'm talking about real hope, a hope for a future filled with happiness and abundance. At first, it truly seems too good to be true. However, you can see the hope in others in sobriety. Some you'll even witness get better right before your eyes and their lives and families restored.

During my years of relapses leading up to me finally getting sober in 2013, I watched many get sober and happy when I could not. I never resented them for that. I may have resented myself, but all that did was push me to want to change, which led me to the beginning of recovery. The witnessing of others getting sober was truly a place of hope to me—a hope that I could have what they were experiencing, a hope that this world of recovery is attainable and realistic, and a hope that I could do this one day at a time. That's another thing that is wonderful about sobriety. If you have even a little bit of faith and hope over the course of each day, anything is possible.

I find hope to be a contagious thing. If you see someone with a powerful sense of hope, I think it starts to affect you personally and may often give you hope as well. Have you ever watched someone or admired someone for having so much hope? You may initially hate them for the same reason. But a tiny part of the back of your brain wishes you, too, could have that hope. Well, you can whether an alcoholic or not. It's simply opening your mind and allowing it to happen. It's a shift in perception. For me, it also involved asking a Higher Power to help me. This doesn't pertain to just drinking. It can be for anything in life. For me, to be open to the idea that something out there had my best interests at heart and was watching over me gave me incredible hope for the future.

Did you ever notice that when you think negatively about something, it tends to happen? Maybe it doesn't happen exactly as your pessimistic thoughts imagined it, but it doesn't seem to turn out positively. I believe there is something to the law of attraction. I bring this up because I think it overlaps with the idea of hope. What you think positively can manifest itself and truly happen in your life. I've seen it happen in my life and in others. A positive attitude mixed with hope has that much power in this world.

The definition of hope is "a feeling of expectation and desire for a certain thing to happen." But what if you changed that sentence to this? A feeling of expectation and desire for a certain positive thing to happen. I'm not trying to change the definition in Webster's Dictionary. I'm simply trying to shift your perception of the word and how to approach it. You do not have to be in recovery for these thoughts to be helpful to you.

How free do you want to be?

1. Have you ever felt truly hopeless?
2. Do you currently feel truly hopeless?
3. Are you willing to change a few things in order to let hope into your life?
4. Do you believe in a Higher Power of any kind?
5. If not, are you willing to believe in something bigger than you?
6. Do you surround yourself with negative people?
7. Do you know some positive people or friends full of hope?
8. Are you willing to be around them more often?

Space to reflect on
hope questions.

"A hope for a future filled with happiness and abundance."

_____

_____

_____

_____

_____

Chapter 3
Faith

Faith may be the most important principle I talk about in this book, so it is a tough one to begin. I guess I'll start with what it was like for me as a kid. My mom's parents had a ton of faith. They brought up my mom in their congregational church. I liked that place. It had a wonderful feel to it. I didn't belong to that church because I lived over an hour away, but I had been baptized there as an infant, as was my brother. We went to a local church. Myself and just a couple of my friends went to this church because the rest of the town was like 98 percent Catholic and we were not. It always bothered me that I couldn't go to church with the rest of my friends in the town that I grew up with and played sports with in those early years. As a child, you don't really put much thought into the actual building you go into on Sundays. It's more about who is around you. So I did the deal and went to Sunday school every Sunday while my friends all went to CCD every Wednesday. I'd make fun of them for having to say confession, and they'd make fun of me for having to endure two-hour Sunday services on a day that revolved around football for at least one season of the year. But it was good. I liked that church and the people in it.

I always believed in God, but I was never sure what that meant. I don't necessarily remember ever personally talking to God, but I do remember saying a bunch of structured prayers. I think I just believed in God because my parents did. It seemed to be what we did on Sundays. While in my grandparents' world, their lives actually revolved around the church. I was always intrigued by their deep faith. I was always impressed, too, that it was their own faith. They didn't press it upon you at all or insist that you had to believe exactly as they did. Our church didn't do so either, but later in life, I saw this a lot in churches I attended and tried out for a few Sundays. After being confirmed at the age of thirteen, I don't remember ever setting foot back in the church, except Easter Sundays or the Christmas service. It's just the way it was.

I was a bit of a juvenile delinquent at times all the way through high school and college. I suppose if there was a hole in my soul during those years, I filled it with two things: playing sports and drinking alcohol. Alcohol, once I was like sixteen, pretty much ruled my social life. Every aspect of what I did or the plans I made revolved around alcohol. That lifestyle continued for another twenty years! As an adult, I had glimpses of wanting to have faith and going to a few church services when I lived in North Carolina and some when I moved to Texas. But I never got to the point where I really wanted to go, and I didn't feel like any of the services I attended sparked a relationship between God and myself.

During a few times I went to church, I sat by myself in a pew through the service and simply wept. I couldn't stop drinking, and it ruled my entire universe. I wanted to be a good family person and a dad, but drinking was always involved. I was at a place where I couldn't live with it and I couldn't live without it. This is a critical place for an alcoholic we often refer to as step zero.

When I got sober, I was shown by some others who got sober that I could have my own relationship with God, a God of my own choosing. Many people got sober and had deep resentments about a God they were taught to believe in through their childhood. Many felt God turned His back on them. Many didn't believe anything at all or were agnostic. There were also those who had deep faith in God but couldn't get sober. It was quite apparent early on that we were not to get sober unless we believed in some sort of Higher Power, even if it meant putting your faith in the universe or nature. I had to realize I had been trying to control everything around me my entire life. I was filled with anxiety, and I was scared of everything. For me, I always had a belief in God since I was very little. I don't know why or how to explain it. I just did. I went back to that version of my God and chose this time to have a personal relationship with that God. It's none of my business what others believe in, but I know what I believe in at this point and it grows and matures every day. For me to get sober, it took me to hand it all over to God and Jesus and literally say out loud, "This life, these issues I'm having, this obsession to drink, it's too much for me to handle. I need help." That was the beginning of it all and the start of my faith and my spiritual journey.

When there is a problem in my life that is too heavy, if I'm worrying about something that I cannot control, if I fear something that I can't handle,

I literally in my mind physically hand that to God and ask Him to take it. The mental picture and physical act of handing it to Him changes everything for me, including my perspective. My relationship with God grows year after year of me being sober. I talk to Him every day and ask Him to guide my actions, my thoughts, my words, and my behavior. I also ask Him to help me recognize anyone in my path that may need help.

I'm no Bible scholar. In fact, this is the first year I've ever read it from cover to cover. However, I've always been fascinated with Jesus. He hung out and loved the sinners. Maybe that's why I love Him so much. I don't find that done too often by those that claim to be deeply religious. I think like hope, our faith also has a ripple effect. My youngest daughter took it upon herself to get baptized because it's something she wanted to do, not something someone told her to do. She wanted a new start with God. My wife and I since getting sober put so much effort into praying to the point it no longer seems like effort. I started reminding myself to pray every day when I got sober. Then it just came naturally. Then it was something I enjoyed doing and wanted to do several times per day. They say it takes thirty days to form a habit. Most of my habits are not so great. The habit of prayer might be the best habit I could ever suggest to anyone. It changes who we are and turns us away from being selfish and into becoming selfless and wanting to help others.

The definition of faith is "complete trust or confidence in someone or something." I like that because it used to be me attempting to only trust myself with decisions. That failed in my life. It is such a relief and a comforting feeling to now have complete and utter trust in God. He has saved my life so many times from my own self-imposed crisis and near-death experiences. Maybe if I simply keep doing that, I can avoid most of those mistakes and tragedies. Maybe you could as well.

How free do you want to be?

1. Do you believe in a Higher Power?
2. If not, why? Was it pushed on you as a child?
3. What if you had your own conception of God?
4. If you could pick three things you'd want in your own personal God, what would they be?

5. What if I told you those three things were your starting point to faith?
6. Would you be interested in praying and relying on that Higher Power?
7. Would you be willing to try praying for thirty days every morning to that God you chose?

Space to reflect on
faith questions.

"The habit of prayer
might be the best
habit I could ever
suggest to anyone."

_____

_____

_____

_____

_____

CHAPTER 4
Courage

I believe all men deep down want to have impressive courage. Maybe it is that way with all people. I can only speak for me, and I spent most of my life in utter fear that my solution was to drown myself in alcohol in order to feel brave in all situations. I think we're born with incredible courage, albeit blind bravery. I think when we are young, we don't know the dangers in life quite yet or the things that could truly cause us harm. I mean I remember climbing the highest of trees and taking jumps on my BMX bike that no human should do. I seemed to have feared nothing. But then things happen in our lives where we create or face fear due to an experience. The first major one I can think of was me playing Little League.

I was nearly 100 percent fearless playing that game at seven years old. My brother was three years older than me, so my dad let me practice with their team as early as five years old. I'd field grounders and take infield practice, shag fly balls, and take a few swings at the plate. I don't remember ever being scared up to that point, and I felt I was made to play that game. All I wanted to do was play for the Boston Red Sox.

I finally arrived at the age where I could play Little League, around eight years old. We had an exhibition game against a neighboring town. I remember seeing the pitcher on the mound warming up, and he looked huge to me because he was twelve. My cocky brain really thought I was going to show him. It was my turn to shine. On the first time I faced him at the plate, I dug my cleats in and was ready to hit a single, probably the best I could accomplish as a scrawny, little kid of that age. About two pitches in, he sailed one up high and inside. For what reason I don't know, I turned the opposite way to get out of the way of the pitch, even though my dad had taught me for years how to get out of the way or turn back to the pitcher. It was too late. That fastball, even at that level of play, hit me square in the face and did some serious damage. It shattered my orbital bone, and I was taken off the field and rushed to the hospital. I remember being so upset that I had to be taken out of the game. I didn't realize how big of an impact that would have on me later. My dad, being the good person he is, told me I didn't have to play again if I didn't want to do so. I guess he knew something I didn't. I almost didn't understand the option. Not play baseball? What an insane proposition.

But then came the day I had to stand back in the batter's box again. You would have thought the pitcher was throwing knives at me. Luckily, the pitcher I was facing was a good friend of the family, John Hutchinson. I'm thankful to this day for that guy. He knew how nervous I was, and he was sort of just lobbing meatballs at me. I hit a single to right field. But that fear never left, and I never batted the same again all throughout my years of baseball through the age of eighteen.

I tell this story because it's impactful moments like that in our lives that cause these fears that we didn't have originally. Most of them are more subtle than that one, of course, but they are still there. Life can be a scary place, and we start to not only have legitimate fears at times but we create these irrational fears about the future regarding things that likely will never happen to us. Alcohol cured all these fears, at least while I was young. Later in life, fast forward fifteen years, alcohol had less of an overall effect. By this, I mean that those fears subsided while drinking, but the morning after brought on more irrational fears and anxiety than one can even fathom. At that stage, I was just drinking to forget the fear and stuff it down inside.

It seems most of us who are trying to recover from something always have this hole inside us. Deep down, we have fears, regrets, resentments, etc. So instead of finding a healthy way to identify these fears and deal with them, we stuff them down and pour alcohol on top of them. This remedy of cocktails and hangovers does nothing to produce courage. If anything, it creates a false reality. True alcoholics start to think their life is normal and that living in a fantasy world of temporary drunken relief followed by morning and days of shame and guilt is acceptable. The question becomes this: If you give up alcohol, what do you now put in that hole in your soul? This is again where spirituality or a belief in a Higher Power comes into play.

Men of faith always seem to have an abundance of courage. I admire that. It's subtle, and it's quiet courage—never boasting or being loud about it. I watched others who were sober have incredible

27

peace who seemed 100 percent calm in the middle of life's storms. I wanted that. I craved that. I wanted peace so bad, so I'd ask them how to get there. They'd tell me to surrender, to turn things over to a Higher Power, something bigger than me. I heard a lot of people with long-term sobriety say, "All you need to know about God right now is that you're not Him." I went back to believing in the God I had as a child. It started there, grew, and matured.

Since letting go and letting God, I no longer have to be in control. It's a paradox that surrendering is a sign of weakness, but yet in sobriety, it's a way to strength. I was told early in sobriety that I cared too much about what people thought of me. That was a fear that consumed me. At nine years sober, that often never creeps into my mind anymore.

It's a funny thing because if you're living an honest life and you're always doing the next right thing, you no longer have to worry what people are thinking of you. If you know God truly loves you, the courage you had as a child is restored. But imagine having that courage and then some mixed with all your life's experiences. You could then turn your life into a world of being of service to others, showing them what sobriety or freedom from any addiction has done for you and opening their eyes to having courage too.

This belief in a Higher Power goes beyond sobriety. It can bring anyone courage that they've lost over the years. The dictionary's definition of courage is this: The ability to do something that frightens you or strength in the face of pain or grief.

Isn't it a wonderful thought that maybe believing in a power greater than yourself could gain you this in life?

How free do you want to be?

1. Do you suffer from the same fears year after year?
2. What initially caused these fears?
3. Do you think any of these fears are real or is it possible they're just in your mind?
4. What would you be willing to do to escape these fears?
5. Do you believe in a Higher Power?
6. If not, are you willing to believe in something bigger than yourself?

Space to reflect on
courage questions.

"Men of faith
always seem to
have an abundance
of courage."

_____

_____

_____

_____

_____

CHAPTER 5
Integrity

When I look up the definition of integrity, it says, "The quality of being honest and having strong moral principles—moral uprightness." When I first got sober, an older and much wiser gentleman said to me, "You know what integrity is? It's when you do something for someone, but you never seek any recognition for it. It can also mean doing something nice for someone and not taking credit for it." I had to think back, way back, to understand if I was truly doing that or not.

Throughout my life, I've always tried to be nice to people and do things to help them. But the question really is this: Did I want credit for doing those things, and did I want someone to know publicly that I did those things? I would say looking back that half the time, I did it for solid reasons and just did it out of the goodness of my heart. However, the older I got and the more I consumed alcohol, it seems to me the pattern was to always let people know what I had done for someone else. I wanted people to see me as a good person, someone they could count on.

As I mentioned in the previous chapter, it's been told to me many times that I care too much about what people think of me. If that is true, I was clearly trying to inflate my level of self-worth to make me personally feel better. I only seemed to feel better if everyone liked me. That is an impossible place to live. It's 100 percent unrealistic to think that everyone is going to like you or approve of you. So here is where the change of perception comes in.

If you're living a good life and simply doing the next right thing day after day, you never have to worry about what people think of you. This is because you, God, and the closest people around you recognize that you are genuine. This is by no means implying that you won't make mistakes and want recognition from time to time, but it shows that you're human and you're being your authentic self.

Integrity in sobriety is brought to your attention very quickly if you surround yourself with the right people. I think that is a very smart step toward both learning and emulating integrity in your life. You should begin by surrounding yourself with integrity. For me, that started by hanging around people that had been sober a very long time. It also meant surrounding myself with people that had something within them that I craved or wanted. For me personally, that usually looked like a sense of peace or an aura of being calm. If you had that look or that persona, I stuck to you like glue at the beginning, hoping I could catch whatever you had and let it rub off on me a little. So that's what I did and that's who I hung around with when I got sober.

One of those guys first taught me that I need to be reliable.

He had asked me one night, "Hey, you going to Denny's with us on Friday night?"

I replied, "Maybe."

His response was "Well, when an alcoholic says maybe, they actually mean no. So let me know if you change your mind."

I was confused. I think I honestly meant maybe. I don't know, but the more I thought about it, the more I realized maybe was always a way out because I had already started convincing myself that I didn't want to go for various reasons in my warped, waterlogged brain. What he was teaching me was to be responsible and true to my word. If you want to go, tell the person, "Yes, I'll be there." However, if any part of you does not want to go, you can say, "You know what? I'm just not up for it. I'll meet you next time." So again, this takes us back to principle number one: Just be honest!

Honesty is a huge factor in having integrity: being somewhere when someone expects you to be, showing up when someone asks for help, and being dependable in every sense of the word. We didn't have the capability of being true to our word in our drunken world, but now we can! We can actually be responsible human beings at this point. We can mean what we say and say what we mean. What a revelation.

The other factor to having integrity for me is being able to admit when we're wrong. A sober person once said to me early in my recovery, "Would you rather be right or would you rather be happy?" Powerful words for me to hear. The truth is we'd rather be both. But what are the chances of that in an argument?

In sobriety, we're taught to stop fighting with people. It's not worth it. It doesn't mean you can't stand up for yourself. Quite the contrary. In fact, now that we're living right and sober, we'll never be a doormat for anyone ever again. However, what it's talking about is being able to walk away from a useless fight—when it truly doesn't matter proving you're right if it's going to ruin the relationship with that other person. Many of these things mentioned can bring you to have a bit of integrity. It certainly isn't an overnight process. It takes work. But like anything else, practice doesn't make perfect. Practice makes permanent. Why not practice the right things and permanently have some integrity?

How free do you want to be?

1. Do you always put yourself first?
2. Do you always seek recognition for something you did?
3. Do you find you always have to be right?
4. If so and you fail in doing so, does it eat you up for weeks?
5. Can you admit when you're wrong?
6. Do you have the ability to walk away from an argument?
7. When you tell someone that you'll be somewhere, do you 100 percent of the time show up?

Space to reflect on
integrity questions.

"Why not practice
the right things
and permanently
have some
integrity?"

_____

_____

_____

_____

_____

CHAPTER 6
Willingness

I think for alcoholics, it's been said that we move at the speed of pain. I've been willing to do a lot of things in my life. Some of them were detrimental to my health, some were fun, some were a learning experience. But at no time in my twenty-five-year drinking career was I willing, or even remotely thinking about being willing, to stop consuming alcohol. Alcohol always did what I asked it to do until it didn't. Willingness is the key to taking action and is necessary to make the changes necessary to live freely.

I remember being completely unwilling to even think of going to rehab or a treatment center. I think that is because if I agreed to do that, either I'd lose my job or it would be the end of my fun forever. I mean who would be willing to do that? But the pain had so outweighed the fun that it was getting to the point that I had to get willing to do something different. I mean without knowing it, I had clearly been willing to neglect my kids, ruin relationships, make my parents worry about me constantly, not put 100 percent into my job, let my health deteriorate, and isolate from everybody. Was I so willing to do all those things but yet not get help? Simply put, I was an alcoholic who was not willing to stop drinking. But with enough warnings from my doctor and a frightening trip to the ER, I knew I had to be willing to change in some way.

The first attempt was to go to rehab on my path to recovery. To be completely honest, it was a great treatment center and I learned quite a bit about myself. I spent twenty-eight days there, and I came home and wasn't willing to change much about my life at all, except eliminate alcohol. This meant my routines didn't change. It meant I still hung out with the same circle of people. I kept the same hobbies. That approach will only take you so far. You have to be willing to put in the work to defend yourself against your own brain that will convince you to drink once again. It will also convince you that maybe you over-exaggerated your drinking problem. My wife always says it best that she has a brain that wants to kill her body. I can think of no better description than that because without a program to stop drinking and the willingness to fill that spiritual hole with something new besides alcohol, you will go back to drinking if you're a true alcoholic.

I got out of rehab after almost a month, and I got complacent. Within five months, I convinced myself that I wasn't an alcoholic and circumstances were what made me drink. I thought maybe if I just drank to the level that kept me out of rehab, I could finally control it. I attempted this off and on for roughly five weeks until once again, I was almost in the ER. That was my last bout with drinking back in 2013. I got a few days sober, and my willingness came in one form. I decided I would do whatever it takes to never go back to rehab again. That's how it started. If that was the willingness to kick off this new way of life, then so be it. That was enough to open the door to serenity.

I joined a twelve-step program and decided to get honest with everyone, to be open with everyone, and to be willing to do what it took to be happy again. Because that was the thing with me. I hadn't yet been happy sober. I'd had moments of peace, but I hadn't had true happiness.

In the middle of all these decisions, I was selling my home that I couldn't afford anymore and I was downsizing to a smaller home. I was approaching fifty thousand in debt and just getting back on my feet again. When I bought that new house, I swore that I'd never drink in that home. I still haven't nine years later. I know they say a geographic change won't help you stop drinking. They are likely correct, but this change of address definitely had an impact on me. My past house just had too many demons in it, hidden bottles, and negative energy. So here I was in a new home, a new drive to stay sober, and a yearning for peace and happiness.

I was willing to admit I was a true alcoholic and would do anything to stay sober. I surrounded myself with sober people, built a powerful sober circle, worked a solid program, and mainly did a lot of things differently than I had ever done ever before. In the middle of all this, God brought a woman into my life that I immediately knew was going to be my best friend. I had no idea she would be the catalyst to a brand-new world of positive energy and become the soul mate I thought I'd never find.

Willingness is the key to it all. All you need to do is pick up that key to open the door. The door is to a lifestyle you've never dreamed of, a spirituality you likely thought you'd never find, and a happiness that is sustainable.

Willingness in the dictionary says "the quality or state of being prepared to do something—readiness." I like that definition, especially the readiness part.

How free do you want to be?

1. Are you ready to make a change?
2. Are you willing to admit you're an alcoholic or have some other issue that is holding you back from living the life you want?
3. What aspects of your life are you willing to give up?
4. Would you do anything to be healthy and happy?
5. What are some things you are not willing to accept or change in your life?
6. Are you willing to lose your life or your family?
7. How free do you want to be?

Space to reflect on
willingness questions.

*"Willingness is the
key to it all. All
you need to do is
pick up that key to
open the door."*

_____

_____

_____

_____

_____

CHAPTER 7
Humility

The dictionary definition of humility is a modest or low view of one's own importance. I don't know if that's the best way to describe it, but I understand the phrasing of that. I heard someone else give a phenomenal description of it that really made much more sense. I can't remember for the life of me who actually said it or if it's actually a famous quote. He or she said that humility is not thinking less of yourself but thinking of yourself less. I believe that definition 100 percent describes the complete psychic change that an alcoholic goes through when working a program to get sober. I don't think one can be happy in sobriety or really learn to perceive the world differently until they gain some humility. The humorous part about humility is that the moment you tell someone you have it, don't you lose it? I suppose it's just living in humility and people seeing in your actions that you've become a better person.

When I first got sober, I remember being in a conversation with some other sober people and somehow, the subject of charity work came up. I proudly told them that I had delivered groceries to the elderly for Meals on Wheels once a month for the past decade. Maybe it was the way I said it that came off egomaniacal. I'm not sure. But one of the gentlemen said back to me, "I bet you tell people so it makes you look good and you can feel really good about yourself!" The comment kind of pissed me off. In my head at the time, I truly thought I was doing a good deed and it had nothing to do with ego. Maybe part of that was true. My intentions were probably somewhat good, as I knew deep down that I was doing a good deed to help the elderly by volunteering.

However, what were my motives behind that? I can't quite remember, but I do know that I told quite a few people about it. What would have been the harm in not telling anyone and just knowing myself that I was trying to help people? Instead, I took great pride in telling anyone that would listen. I think I also did it because I was living such an awful life that I needed to do something good in order to make myself feel like I was living a normal and productive life.

For years, I was not living with any true value or ethics and alcohol was slowly but surely ridding me of any soul I had left. To me personally, getting sober was the first step in the journey of getting back to what God created me to be in the first place. I think the longer we're sober, the more we have clarity and the closer we get to having pure motives.

None of us are perfect. But we do get better and it's okay to notice we're getting better. That's the part where we no longer think less of ourselves. The tricky part is thinking of ourselves less. How does one do this? A twelve-step program taught me to always get out of my own head. As alcoholics, we've got a brain that wants to kill our body as my wife always says. So why not rid yourself of delusional thoughts or detrimental thinking patterns by doing things for others. That could mean reaching out to people who need your help in any way you can. When I say that, I mean it could be anyone. It could be someone in recovery, a friend, a relative, or even a stranger in the street.

Our whole lives, I feel like our goal should be that if we cross paths with anyone on any given day, we make their lives a little bit better by seeing or talking to us. This could be just reaching out to see how someone is doing. It could also be as small as smiling at a stranger who looks like they may need it. Thinking of ourselves less is paramount to growing as a person. In many ways, this spirit of service not only helps those in need but it helps us. It makes us less selfish and puts love back into the world. I find that to be an amazing opportunity.

I don't think we realize the ability we have as humans to change someone's day just by being kind. We have so many opportunities on every single day to help someone or change their outlook about themselves. However, we get so stuck in our own heads that we don't notice what is going on around us or who needs our assistance. I encourage anyone to go out and try to really take it all in on any given day. Challenge yourself to watch everything going on around you and out in the world for an entire day while also not drifting into thoughts about yourself or your situations. You'll start to see the world differently.

How free do you want to be?

1.   Do you think of yourself all day?

2. Do those thoughts of yourself consist of regret for the past or worry of the future?
3. Do you wish to get out of that mindset?
4. Are you willing to be of service to others?
5. How does it make you feel to help others in need?
6. Do you immediately have to tell others about the help you gave to someone?

Space to reflect on
humility questions.

"Humility is
not thinking
less of yourself
but thinking of
yourself less."

_____

_____

_____

_____

_____

CHAPTER 8
Love

I feel like there are so many directions I can go with the principle of love. As I said in my previous book on relationships, "Love is everything and it changes and shifts, and it grows." I still believe and live in that world. I guess let's start with the definition of love. It states that love is an intense feeling of deep affection. I think that's a good start on the definition, but how could the word love be explained in such few words? I don't think it can.

Love has such an impact on an alcoholic when getting sober. We're sometimes described as ego maniacs with an inferiority complex. That is or was a perfect description of me at the end of my drinking. Here I was, trying to make everyone think I was okay or that I was functioning fine, but inside, I was falling apart and the world outside me was starting to follow suit. I was a mess. I tried so hard to put on a happy face and show this bravado, but really, I was riddled with insecurities.

When you get into recovery, it truly is about acceptance and finding a way to love yourself. But what's great about a twelve-step program is that like-minded people who have experienced sobriety before you will show you love before you can love yourself. What a concept that truly is. They get to love you when you don't have the capability to do so. This has been happening in the world of recovery for a long time, and it continues to pay itself forward. Now that I've been sober for nine years here in 2022, I must show love to those new in sobriety so that they can find their way as well.

Once we feel that inside and start to acknowledge it as true, we now need to find love from a Higher Power. I happen to choose to call my Higher Power God. God has always loved me. I believed in God. I just simply put Him on the back burner in my life for twenty-plus years. Maybe I was too embarrassed by my actions to face Him. Maybe I thought He'd stop loving me if He knew the things I had experienced or done leading me to the mess I was in right before I got sober. Those in recovery show us that nothing else kept us from drinking. So why not accept God back into our lives and ask Him for help?

Many people I know in recovery are or were very self-sufficient and independent people. Many were raised to get by on their own and never depend on anyone. However, it becomes abundantly clear that we cannot stop drinking ourselves. It may be the one thing that a true alcoholic cannot do alone. It will drive an alcoholic into insanity or death if they don't attempt to get help. I asked other people in recovery for help who had done it before me. If it were not for them, I'm not sure I would have turned my face back to God and received the love from Him that was always there. I'm so glad I did, as it saved my life. It also hit the reset button on a journey back to what God created me to be in the first place.

What I love about this journey and this principle is that it never ends. It's a constant seeking of joy and abundance in our lives tied with the spirit of service and helping others. What a concept for happiness!

So that brings us to loving others, or brotherly love. It's not always easy to do. But once we love ourselves, we can see ourselves in others. Being in recovery has the outstanding privilege of allowing ourselves to see the similarities we have with others, not the differences. Once you can look at a person and see the similarities, it's a game changer. I think that's the first step in achieving or giving love back to that person. When someone is mean or cruel to you, it's much more about them and how they feel rather than it being a reflection of you. Once you realize that and once you can put yourself in their shoes, you can relate and be kind to them.

Love is kind. The longer we live our lives with this mindset, we realize the impact we can have on other people. We can make their day better. The hope is they can feel the love we're giving and maybe it will make them feel at ease. There is no better feeling than love to me. The closest thing I can think of is peace. But I think peace is a byproduct of love. I've never felt more at peace than I have when I was in love, felt love for my family or friends, and also felt the love of God that was watching over me. Some say God is love. If that's true, then I should be seeking Him in all I do on any given day. I try, but none of us are perfect. I just know that love makes us all better people and we truly need more of it in the world right now. I challenge anyone reading this to start making love the focus of your life, not anger or hate. Love everyone, and I mean everyone.

Love shouldn't be compartmentalized for those that treat us well. The biggest impact love can have is on our enemies or with those that we don't get along with very well. Imagine a scenario where you have the power to change things. Imagine a person who may be an enemy or foe, and on the next time you see him or her, you respond with love rather than hate. You may very well have an impact on that person immediately going forward. They may in turn bring that love to someone else and change their day as well. Think of the ripple effect love can have on the human race if we all practiced it.

How free do you want to be?

1. Can you describe how you feel or understand love?
2. Do you love yourself?
3. Do you love just those people that are kind to you?
4. Do you believe in a Higher Power?
5. If so, do you believe this Higher Power loves you?
6. Are you willing to show love to your enemies?

7. How willing are you to make an effort going forward to show all people and creatures love in this world?

Space to reflect on love questions.

"Love is everything
and it changes
and shifts, and
it grows."

_____

_____

_____

_____

_____

_____

CHAPTER 9
Responsibility

Responsibility is what our parents have been trying to teach us since the day we were born. It's something we were taught to strive for: to be responsible young adults. We all fell short, and we learned a lot of lessons along the way. I found two definitions of responsibility. One was the state or fact of being accountable or to blame for something. The second one was the opportunity or ability to act independently and make decisions without authorization. I like both definitions for different reasons, and I think they both tied into my sobriety.

Let's look at these two definitions separately. The first one talks about being accountable or to blame for something. We learn as children early on that when we do something wrong, we get punished or scolded for it. That is not a good feeling. It should change us all to never make that mistake again. But our whole existence is learning new things or taking risks, etc. We continue to make mistakes. If we followed our parents' good advice, we'd say we're sorry or make amends for what we did and not continue that behavior. However, as an alcoholic, I think that is one of our true crossroads where we choose to be responsible, honest adults or lie our asses off to get away with something. Many of us choose to start lying to avoid confrontations or the embarrassment of being caught in a bad situation. But lying and hurting people just fills us with guilt and shame for years to come, even if we were able to dodge punishment in some way. What getting sober does is makes us responsible by being accountable for what we know we've done. It forces us to be honest and face it.

Bringing light into that darkness brings more peace than you can imagine. It does have an element to it of bringing on some anxiety, but making amends to someone you wronged cleans up your side of the street so to speak. It allows you to be responsible for your actions. Making amends to someone should be about you being able to right a wrong that you caused to someone else. It also means you should do this with no expectation of them also making amends to you if you think they were also wrong for something as well. What a concept. Being honest in all areas of life brings on true responsibility. It sets us free and allows us to be the responsible adults that our parents always wanted us to be. It mends relationships, it rebuilds friendships, and it restores love between humans.

The second definition talks about the opportunity or ability to act independently and make decisions without authorization. Alcohol severely warps an alcoholic's brain from years of abusing it where it gets to the point that we live in a world full of delusions. Our decision-making skills are so far gone that we don't know wrong from right or up from down. It leaves us in this state of mind where once we take the alcohol away, it's like having to reprogram our brains.

I can tell you that this is not an overnight affair. Depending on how badly you drank and for how many years, this could be far worse in some people than in others. But many have come into a twelve-step program and barely know how to do the simplest of things once the alcohol is taken away and fear sets in of doing anything right in the world. For many, during this period of the first year of sobriety, we often turn to people with long-term sobriety to help us make our own decisions. This seems extreme, but I assure you it is not. We've convinced ourselves for years or decades that it was our way or the highway. We also think our way of doing things is the only right way. But the reality is those actions and those thoughts only amounted to me being a shell of myself, full of anxiety, and a loss of direction. These wonderful, sober people helped me make some decisions during that time, some big and some small. I couldn't have survived without them.

After living these principles for a good six months, I was able to make wise and responsible decisions once again that made sense not just to me but to the outside world. I think that's about the time that parents, loved ones, employers, and spouses start to tell you they can see a change in clarity in you. They may also say something like "Something has changed in you, but I can't put a finger on what it is." Those moments are miraculous because we can't see it for ourselves. Someone almost needs to point out that change for the better in us.

That to me is where responsibility comes in to play finally in our lives again. We can be there when people need us, we become reliable adults again and we can fess up when we've done something wrong.

How free do you want to be?

1. Are you able to admit when you're wrong?
2. Are you hiding and lying about things in order to avoid accountability?
3. Do you really make wise decisions for yourself?
4. Or have many of your life decisions brought you down a bad path?
5. Do you always show up when you say you will?
6. Are there people you need to make amends to?
7. Are you willing to admit how you've wronged them regardless of their reaction back to you?

Space to reflect on
responsibility questions.

"It mends
relationships,
it rebuilds
friendships, and
it restores love
between humans."

_____

_____

_____

_____

Chapter 10
Discipline

I always thought I had discipline throughout my life. I think as a child, I had some forced discipline. By that I mean, that my parents had me working even before my teen years, my dad got me into sports really young, and I was expected to do certain chores assigned to me by my parents. That's all in the parents' playbook of raising children I suppose. But if our parents hadn't enforced it, would we be truly disciplined without them? I don't know. Maybe. But I think once alcohol entered the picture for me at the age of fourteen or so, all discipline went right out the window. Looking back as a growing alcoholic, you can see the patterns in the life I lived and the directions I went. Any discipline in sports was watered down by my extracurricular drinking. Why would I spend an afternoon of my own time practicing when I could be out drinking with my friends? Why would I put in extra hours at work when I could be going out and tying one on? The introduction of alcohol seemed to put me in this perpetual half-assed mode where I did the bare minimum to get by, including my years in college. I think back to collegiate years, and it's a bit disturbing how little I did beside consume alcohol during those years. Much of it was extremely fun and I had some great times, but anything and everything I did revolved around alcohol. Maybe that's somewhat normal in some ways, but I believe I missed out on a ton by taking that route for 4.5 years.

Once I got sober, it was like retraining my brain to think like a normal human being to remind me to do things that may be simple and everyday things for a normal person. Things like making the bed, paying bills on time, being honest about where you are and where you're going, working hard, and giving as much as you're receiving in life. It's about learning how to be part of and bringing value to the table in your world rather than taking from it or looking to see what you can take.

Sobriety forces you to do a mental checklist in your head every night to see if you wronged anyone, to see if old patterns are coming back, and to make amends quickly and sincerely for anything you may have done wrong on any given day. I imagine normal people don't have to do that. But we do because old patterns and habits die hard. You can't just act all ethical and moral on a daily basis without some practice after drinking for twenty-five years straight in the fashion that I did for so long.

I read the definition of discipline as the practice of training people to obey rules or a code of behavior, using punishment to correct disobedience. I think that's a pretty accurate description when it comes to alcoholics, except there is one flaw to that definition in the world of a problem drinker. It says to obey rules. I find alcoholics are not really keen with the idea of being given rules. Let's call them suggestions instead, shall we? I think if someone suggests something to me, it gives me more of an open mind. It allows me to make the decision to not to be a good person or a jackass. An alcoholic's success is built on the idea of breaking old problematic behaviors that send us down the same bad path all the time. My disease centers in my screwed-up thinking that I lived in for multiple decades.

Giving me a few suggestions to follow is a great thing. Giving me a mental list to go over in my brain to form better behaviors is a good thing.

Why not become disciplined again like God intended us to be in the first place?

How free do you want to be?

1. Do you find yourself at time just putting off things you know you should be doing?
2. Do you think you're capable of change when it comes to your patterns of behavior?
3. Are your everyday habits leaving you productive?
4. Are you a positive person most days?
5. If you set your mind to something, do you do it all the way or half-ass it?
6. What are you willing to do to create some new productive and healthy behaviors?
7. Do you ever review your day?

Space to reflect on
discipline questions.

"It's about learning
how to be part of
and bringing value
to the table in your
world rather than
taking from it or
looking to see what
you can take."

_____

_____

73

Chapter 11
Spirituality

What does spirituality mean to you? Some people believe in God. Some believe in Buddha. Some believe in the Universe or some force of nature. For me, it's a belief in something bigger than me, much bigger. It's too hard not to imagine some kind of Higher Power overseeing it all. This world is so complex and each person so much different from the other. I think I always believed in God since I was a little kid. Part of that is because I went to church a lot as a child and I was pretty sure my parents believed in God. But we were not a really religious family. So where did my strong sense of something watching over me come from? I don't really know, but I think it's born in us. We choose to ignore it or embrace it. Some of us, like me, just put it on the back burner for a very long time. It's hard to go out drinking, act the way I did for so many years, and go home each night and face God with that behavior. It's much easier to say you believe to people, shelve the idea of actually having a relationship with a Higher Power, and act the way you want to without the feeling of being judged. But the problem is we're judging ourselves anyway and often live in guilt and shame all those years. Shoving all those guilty feelings down somewhere for all those years really takes a toll on an alcoholic, and it doesn't end well.

This is where sobriety comes in. Getting sober for me was the difference in believing and having faith in God versus actually trusting God and having a relationship with Him. There is a major difference for me there, so much that it completely changed my life once I decided to look at my life this way. In church, or at least the one I attended, we would say structured prayers during the service. That is to say recited prayers that fit into old traditions. But for me, those structured prayers lacked emotion. They didn't have a personal feeling to them that I could feel in my heart or soul.

What sobriety accomplished was getting me to have a personal relationship with that Higher Power. This was done by simply one day just having a conversation with God, not asking for anything—just a conversation of how I felt at that moment and talking about what I was going through that day. In other words, an actual conversation with God. Imagine that. That changed everything. It became personal. It became real. Now at the very least two times per day I find myself talking to God. That would be right after sitting down with my first cup of coffee every morning, when I'm sitting by myself early in the day before anyone else is awake. I tell God what I'm worried about at that moment. I thank Him for another day alive sober. I pray that He keeps me sober that day. I ask Him to help me through the day by guiding me and matching my will to His. I thank Him for thinking enough of me that He thought I was worthy to be created and walk this earth with so many others. That sets the course of my day and puts it on the right path with no fear. The last time I talk to God on any given day is, of course, at night before I fall asleep. I thank Him for another day of clarity. I thank Him for giving me a chance to walk this earth now in the right way. I tell Him how grateful I am that He didn't give up on me.

At night, it's a lot about gratitude, as I find that necessary to be happy and sleep peacefully. It's not to say I don't talk to God throughout the day, but it isn't planned during those times. Often, it's simply noticing Him in something about the day or a decision made or something that can't be explained naturally that happened that day. It can sometimes just be noticing Him in the beauty of something in my sight. This usually means I look up and smile or hold my hand on my chest for a second and say, *Thank You*, in my head. When you seek, you will find. That discipline of thinking is the game changer. When you start doing that every day, you start to see the world differently.

Then comes the second part of spirituality to me. They say prayer is talking to God. Well, meditation, or at least some sort of silence, is listening to Him. This is a habit and exercise that is going to take some practice. An old-timer suggested I try this after I had been sober for about four years. For the record, I'm now nine years sober, so I guess I've been doing this nearly every day for five years. Meditation opens up a whole new way of living. I'm sure there are a million different ways to meditate. I can only speak from experience, so I will tell you the two ways that I utilize to keep me sane in this world and to keep me centered.

The first is guided meditation. This is simply a person's voice on a recording walking you through a meditation to slow down your brain and to get you concentrating on your breathing. It can also have sound effects like nature or ocean waves or something. I find these are great during the day or at night. If at night, you'll often doze off during it, as you're fatigued from the day. That's fine, as I think part of the purpose of those is to put us to a restful state. So don't feel bad if you fall asleep.

The second kind of meditation to me is just sound, and for me, this meditation is done first thing early in the morning right after I pray or talk to God. I happen to use underwater sounds. I don't know if that's because I grew up around a lot of water, but that is what puts me in the zone for some reason. Trust me. I've tried a lot of sound effects, but it always comes back to water.

I sit quietly, try not to think of much, and concentrate intently on my breathing. You can even count to a certain number breathing in and breathing out to slow yourself down. I often will concentrate on a word when breathing in and then a different word when breathing out. For example, I'll think of the world peace when breathing in and then think of the word fear when breathing out. The idea is that you are bringing peace into yourself on the inhale and breathing out an obstacle or defect on the exhale. If I do this breathing exercise for long enough, I can feel myself almost experiencing a tingling through my arms and I can breathe naturally without thinking the words anymore. I can simply just be but also concentrate on breathing slowly but deeply. I find this pocket of time is when I feel the closest to a Higher Power. Because you've shut everything else off, you're truly listening and shutting off the chatter in your head.

Everyone is different in how they meditate and for how long. I started at three minutes total and worked my way up to thirteen minutes and thirty-one seconds every day. Why that number? I have no idea. But that is where I'm at with meditation at the moment.

I saw this definition of spirituality, and I really like it: Spirituality involves the recognition of a feeling or sense or belief that there is something greater than myself, something more to being human than sensory experience, and that the greater whole of which we are part is cosmic or divine in nature. I can't even expand on that as it's written so close to what I feel or believe. I just know that I get there through prayer, conversations with God, and meditation.

How free do you want to be?

1. Do you believe in a Higher Power of any kind?
2. Do you feel something may be looking out for you that you can't see?
3. What do you do on a daily basis to set the tone for your day?
4. If you believe in God, do you actually pray or do you have personal conversations with God?
5. Can you change the way you practice spirituality or are you too rigid in your thinking?
6. Are you open to meditation?
7. Have you ever been able to slow down the chatter in your brain?
8. Are you willing to open your mind to the concept of a Higher Power?
9. Are you willing to try a few new things in order to find out more about yourself?
10. Do you seek peace in life?

Space to reflect on
spirituality questions.

"When you seek,
you will find."

_____

_____

_____

_____

_____

_____

_____

CHAPTER 12
Service

I think the alcoholic fancies themselves at times the person that is really giving and willing to help everyone around them. In some delusion, they find themselves to be selfless. But if you truly look at their behavior, everything they do involves setting themselves up for the next drink with the least amount of resistance around them. All things that appear to be good deeds that they do are simply done to keep everyone at peace so it will not disturb their world of drinking.

That's not to say that they don't truly like doing good things for people and being generous. I think they do because I was one of them. I truly liked making people happy and going out of my way to help them. But I do think some of that could be done in the sense it makes alcoholics feel good about themselves briefly when internally, they're eating themselves alive with guilt. It also makes them appear to be a good person, which seems to be the outlook most alcoholics want others to think of them. We don't want to be judged unless your opinion is that we are good people. We're a very sensitive bunch. But when we finally get sober and we're taught what real service is, it changes our perception rather quickly. We start to do nice things for others, both for alcoholics and non-alcoholics, and not need recognition for doing so. We do it because it's the right thing to do. We try on a daily basis to help or talk to other alcoholics to check in on each other. We're rather insane sometimes as problem drinkers, but as they say, "We're not all insane on the same day." It helps to look after each other. We truly start to become selfless in many ways.

The only way we still have any selfish action is in the order in which we place priorities in our lives. By this I mean that sobriety has to come first before anything. If we don't put sobriety first, we lose anything we put in front of it. That is why it's so paramount to do things daily to not only work on our sobriety but to never forget that we're alcoholics. Once an alcoholic, always an alcoholic.

With that said, we need to always stay in the middle of the herd so to speak. It doesn't mean that we always have to be helping just the alcoholic. It means we can help anyone in this world and not expect something in return. It's to put other people before ourselves. It's to get out of our own crazy heads, even if it's just for a moment to reach out to someone else who needs a friendly voice. Service work is so important to an alcoholic because it insures our sobriety. I think on a daily basis, there is nothing more important to me and to my sober life than to always accomplish three things. I always need to pray and talk to God. I always need to meditate. And I always need to reach out or talk to another alcoholic or to help someone in need.

If you can do those things daily, it slowly changes how you think and shifts perception. I think it shifts our perception back to what we were always supposed to be before our mistakes, bad habits, and disease got in our way and put us on a path for destruction. It allows us to be human beings at peace—human beings that can feel love and bring value to this world.

How free do you want to be?

1. Do you try to help someone besides your-self every day?
2. Do you have ulterior motives?
3. Do you do things for others to get some-thing out of them?
4. When is the last time you reached out to someone you suddenly thought of?
5. Are you mad when you don't get something in return?
6. Does your intuition tell you to call some-one but you ignore it?
7. Do you feel instantly better when you help someone?

Space to reflect on
service questions.

"It's to get out
of our own crazy
heads, even if it's
just for a moment to
reach out to someone
else who needs a
friendly voice."

_____

_____

_____

CONCLUSION

I've sat for months trying to think how to conclude this book. I'll start by saying I'm forever grateful for this sober life. There are too many people to thank personally, but there are many in the recovery community and my family that were a part of saving my life. The only way that I can repay that debt is to pass on what was given to me so freely years ago. Those in recovery shared their story with me so I could relate. The way for me to truly pay it forward is to tell my story and help others that are still suffering.

I went into this world of recovery to stop the pain and to stop a life that was spiraling out of control. I wanted to look into my parents' eyes and not see worry or fear about what may happen to me. I wanted my kids to look up to me again and be able to give them a parent that was truly present. I wanted to find true love or at least love myself again. I wanted to be a responsible employee and have people rely on me once again. I wanted the anxiety and guilt to go away and never return. I wanted hope. More than anything, I simply wanted to be happy.

What I got was a playbook for how to live. I didn't realize what would come with that new way of life. It brought these twelve principles to me and taught me how to incorporate them into my world. I was likely taught many of these same principles by my parents when I was a child, but alcohol erased them temporarily and this way of life brought them back alive. Once you practice these principles, they start to become part of who you are and how you want to be in this world. I think the only real way to pay something forward is to show or tell someone how you experienced it. There is a truth in that approach that gives it power. I've always learned more from hearing someone tell me a story about situations that they experienced themselves. That sense of being able to relate to someone or something is the game changer. It makes us realize it's possible for us as well. It makes us realize that the storyteller isn't full of shit. I think that part is important. I would not have written this book had I not experienced all of it. Am I really great at practicing all these principles? No, not exactly. But living right and following these principles is as progressive as the disease of alcoholism or any addiction can be.

I don't want you or anyone else suffering to have to experience it any longer than you have already. You can change. You can recover. It doesn't even have to be alcoholism you suffer from in life. These principles can apply anywhere and everywhere. Do you believe me? The fact is I believe in you, I think your world can change, and you can truly live abundantly and have daily gratitude for it all. You may even find love. Most importantly, you might start to love yourself again, and the truth is that it all starts right there. How free do you want to be?

About the Author

 Dean Anderson is forty-nine years of age, has been sober for nine years, and has started this journey of recovery on February 7, 2013. He came from the small town of Lakeville, Massachusetts, and now lives in Austin, Texas. His drinking life started at the age of thirteen and ended at the age of thirty-nine. He was at a point where he could not live with alcohol, nor could he live without it. He was on the brink of death and emotionally and spiritually bankrupt.

After twenty-five years living with the progressive illness of alcoholism, he had to find a way out or die. The life of a true alcoholic never gets better while continuing to drink. It simply gets worse until one has the willingness to get help. It took him years to ask for this assistance. He could not understand why he was independently able to conquer or accomplish most things in his life on his own, but his drinking problem he could not. He had to come to grips with the fact that he could not do this alone and needed the help of others who had experienced the same problem.

In 2013, he surrendered to the idea that he truly was an alcoholic and needed to take some action to get sober and start a new life. Through the mentorship of others, he learned a playbook for living that included twelve principles: honesty, hope, faith, courage, integrity, willingness, humility, love, responsibility, discipline, spirituality, and service. These things allowed him to become the person he was always meant to be. They also resulted in him having the happiest life he's ever experienced. After receiving all these gifts of recovery, he wanted to help as many people find what he found on this journey. He figured, along with personally helping alcoholics locally, he could write a book for all to read. This book contains these principles that saved his life so that the people who read this book can do the same thing for themselves or pass it on to their loved ones experiencing this disease. He truly hopes it inspires many to get sober.